Endpapers:
Detail from picture stone,
Museum of National Antiquities,
Stockholm

shirley glubok

the art of the vikings

DESIGNED BY GERARD NOOK

MACMILLAN PUBLISHING CO., INC.
New York
COLLIER MACMILLAN PUBLISHERS
London

Viking swords,
The National Museum
of Denmark, Copenhagen

To Mildred Baker and Katharine Oliver

The author gratefully acknowledges the assistance of:
Bertil Almgren, Professor of Northern European Prehistory, Uppsala University; *Björn Ambrosiani*, Keeper of the Museum Department, Museum of National Antiquities, Stockholm; *Helge Braathen*, Curator, Archaeological Museum, Stavanger; *Arne Emil Christensen, Jr.*, First Curator, University Museum of National Antiquities, Oslo; *Hakon Christie*, Architect, National Antiquarian Office, Oslo; *Raghnall Ó Floinn*, Irish Antiquities Division, National Museum of Ireland, Dublin; *Ann Stine Ingstad*; *Elisabeth Munksgaard*, Assistant Keeper, The National Museum of Denmark, Copenhagen; *Maj Odelberg*, Curator, Museum of National Antiquities, Stockholm; *Thorkild Ramskou*, Curator, The National Museum of Denmark; *Breandán Ó Ríordáin*, Keeper, National Museum of Ireland and Director of the Viking-Medieval excavations in Old Dublin; *Astrid Sjöberg*, Curator, Museum of National Antiquities, Stockholm; *Leo Jakobson*, junior adviser; and especially the helpful cooperation of *Bente Magnus* and *Björn Myhre*, Archaeologists, Historical Museum, University of Bergen.

Macmillan Publishing Co., Inc., 866 Third Avenue, New York, N.Y. 10022
Collier Macmillan Canada, Ltd.
Printed in the United States of America

10 9 8 7 6 5 4 3 2 1

LIBRARY OF CONGRESS CATALOGING IN PUBLICATION DATA

Glubok, Shirley.   The art of the Vikings.   SUMMARY: A survey of the art and culture of the Norsemen from approximately 800 A.D. to approximately 1100 A.D. 1. Art, Viking—Juvenile literature. [1. Art, Viking] I. Nook, Gerard. II. Title.

N6275.G58   1978   709'.02   78-6849   ISBN 0-02-736460-7

Silver figure, Museum of National Antiquities, Stockholm

almost everyone has heard of the Vikings, but few people know who they really were. The people we call Vikings were from Norway, Sweden and Denmark, the northernmost area of Europe, known as Scandinavia. About 800 A.D. some of these Norsemen, or Northmen, began to leave their homelands and sail to foreign shores to trade, raid, explore and settle. To the west they crossed the North Sea and Atlantic Ocean to Ireland, Britain, Iceland, Greenland and even North America. To the east they sailed down the great rivers of Russia to the Black and Caspian seas, and they went as far south as North Africa. This period when the Norsemen went adventuring lasted about 250 years, and is called the Viking Age.

Although the word "Viking" usually has stood for those fearless raiders who went to sea, most Norsemen were peaceful farmers, traders and craftsmen. As a people they admired generosity, hospitality and loyalty. They were powerful and courageous; they excelled in battle and had no fear of death.

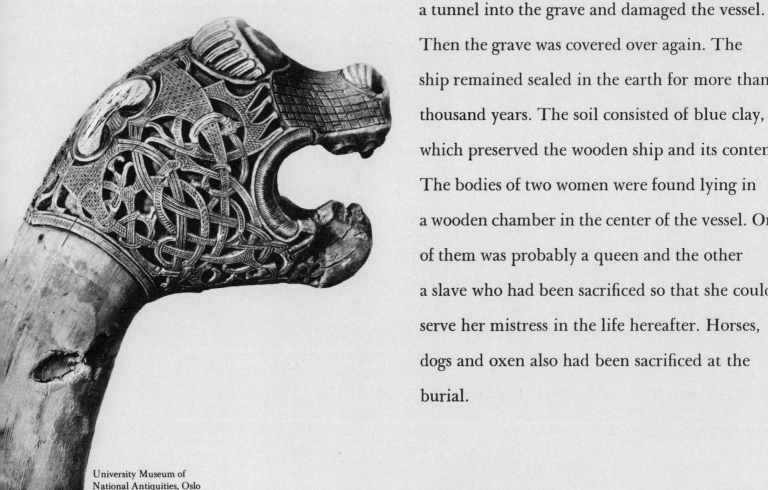

Scandinavia is almost surrounded by water, with the North Sea on one side, the Baltic Sea on the other, and many lakes and rivers in between. The people have always been skillful seamen and shipbuilders. Viking vessels were masterpieces of wood carving. Some boats were made for war, others for peaceful trading, some for sailing on rivers and along coasts, others for crossing the dangerous ocean.

Sometimes boats were used for burial. In Norway in the Viking Age a yacht, or luxury boat, was dragged onto the land on what is now the Oseberg farm and buried with its owner. The ship was covered with a mound of earth. Shortly after the burial, robbers dug a tunnel into the grave and damaged the vessel. Then the grave was covered over again. The ship remained sealed in the earth for more than a thousand years. The soil consisted of blue clay, which preserved the wooden ship and its contents. The bodies of two women were found lying in a wooden chamber in the center of the vessel. One of them was probably a queen and the other a slave who had been sacrificed so that she could serve her mistress in the life hereafter. Horses, dogs and oxen also had been sacrificed at the burial.

University Museum of
National Antiquities, Oslo

The carved animal head on a short post, at left, was found with the Oseberg ship. Animals were the favorite subjects of Viking artists.

The Oseberg ship is light and flexible. She is constructed with long narrow planks of oak that overlap each other and are held together with iron rivets, or bolts. She was steered by a large rudder. The Vikings had no compass or charts; they navigated by the sun and stars.

The stern, or rear end, of the Oseberg ship rises in a graceful curve ending in a spiral, like a coiled serpent. Fine decorations of long, twisting animal figures are carved into the wood. This boat was made for sailing in coastal waters; she was not sturdy enough to cross the ocean.

University Museum of
National Antiquities, Oslo

everything that the owner might need in the life hereafter had been buried with the Oseberg ship: beautiful sleds, beds with quilts and pillows, two tents, kitchen utensils, wool and silk cloth, as well as the wagon below. It is thought that jewelry had also been buried with the women but had been stolen when the grave was robbed.

The wagon was probably used for ceremonies. Figures carved on the front may represent the legend of Gunnar in the snake pit. Gunnar and his brother were invited to a feast by their brother-in-law, who knew that Gunnar owned a treasure of gold.

University Museum of
National Antiquities, Oslo

The invitation was a trap to capture the brothers and seize the treasure. Gunnar was warned of the plot, but he wanted to go anyway. He and his brother hid the treasure in a river and went to the feast. When they arrived, they were seized. Gunnar was told that his life would be saved if he would reveal where the treasure was hidden. Fearful that his brother might tell, Gunnar demanded that he be given his brother's heart. Now he was the only one who knew the secret. He still refused to tell, and was thrown alive into a snake pit to struggle with the reptiles forever.

The head at right was carved over a front wheel of the wagon.

In Denmark, in the Roskilde fjord, or deep inlet, five ships had been loaded with stones and sunk, probably to block the channel when the Norsemen were attacked by enemies from the sea. One of the sunken vessels was a typical Viking longship, or warship. Others were bulky cargo boats called knarrs, used for trading. The wooden planking at right is from one of the knarrs.

University Museum of
National Antiquities, Oslo

The Viking Ship Museum,
Roskilde, Denmark

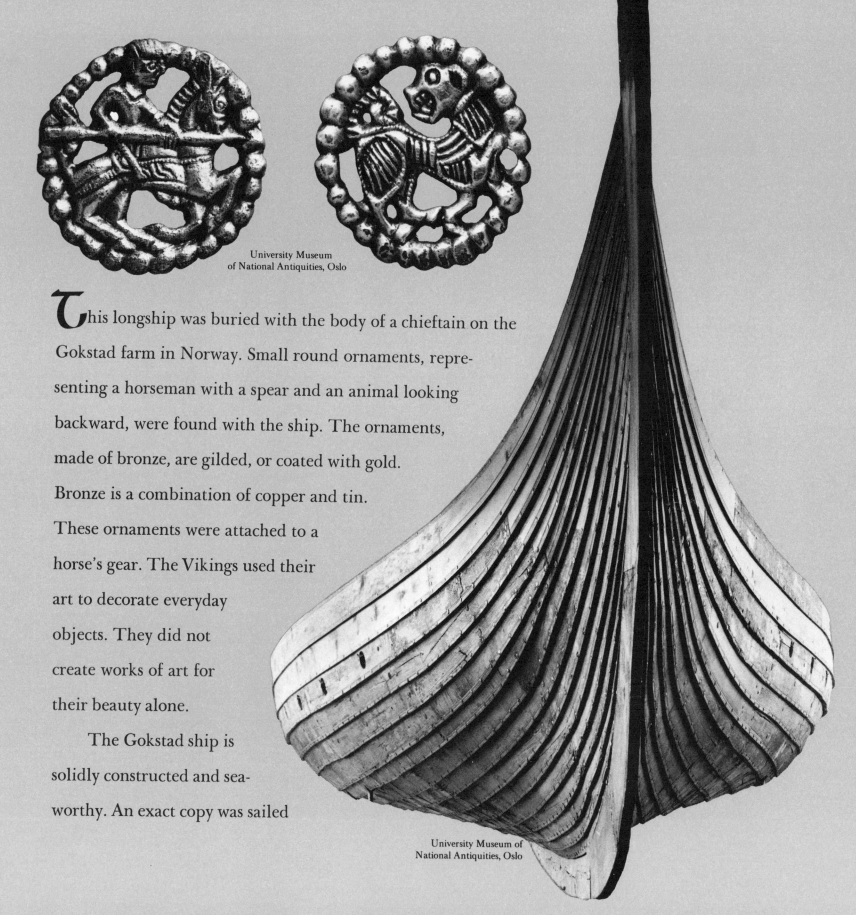

This longship was buried with the body of a chieftain on the Gokstad farm in Norway. Small round ornaments, representing a horseman with a spear and an animal looking backward, were found with the ship. The ornaments, made of bronze, are gilded, or coated with gold. Bronze is a combination of copper and tin. These ornaments were attached to a horse's gear. The Vikings used their art to decorate everyday objects. They did not create works of art for their beauty alone.

The Gokstad ship is solidly constructed and seaworthy. An exact copy was sailed across the Atlantic Ocean in 1893 for the World's Fair in Chicago. In spite of stormy weather, the voyage took only twenty-eight days.

The vessel has sixteen oar holes on each side so that she could be rowed when there was no wind to fill the sails. Shields were found between the oar holes. These would be hung on the sides of the vessel for display when the ship was in a harbor.

Skeletons of a dozen horses, half a dozen dogs and even a peacock were found with the ship, as well as three small boats, oars, beds, a sled and kitchen utensils. The flat animal head at right is from the post of a bed. Perhaps the figure was supposed to frighten away evil spirits. Its pointed ears stick straight up and it has large teeth.

University Museum of
National Antiquities, Oslo

9

The Vikings were able to carry off their raids on foreign shores because their ships were light and swift; the vessels were built so they could sail in shallow coastal waters and could be pulled ashore easily. Viking warriors struck quickly and fled before their victims had time to organize a defense.

Museum of National Antiquities, Stockholm

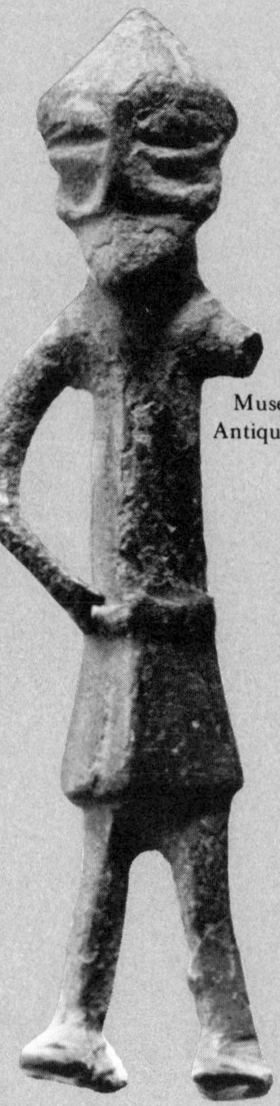

Norse chieftains wore pointed helmets made of iron or leather, with a metal bar extending over the nose. The small figure at right, representing Odin, the Norse god of war, wisdom and magic, wears a simple pointed helmet with a nose guard. Odin is shown with a mustache and short beard, which were stylish at that time.

A Swedish Viking wearing his helmet is represented at left. The head was carved on the end of an elk antler.

Museum of National Antiquities, Stockholm

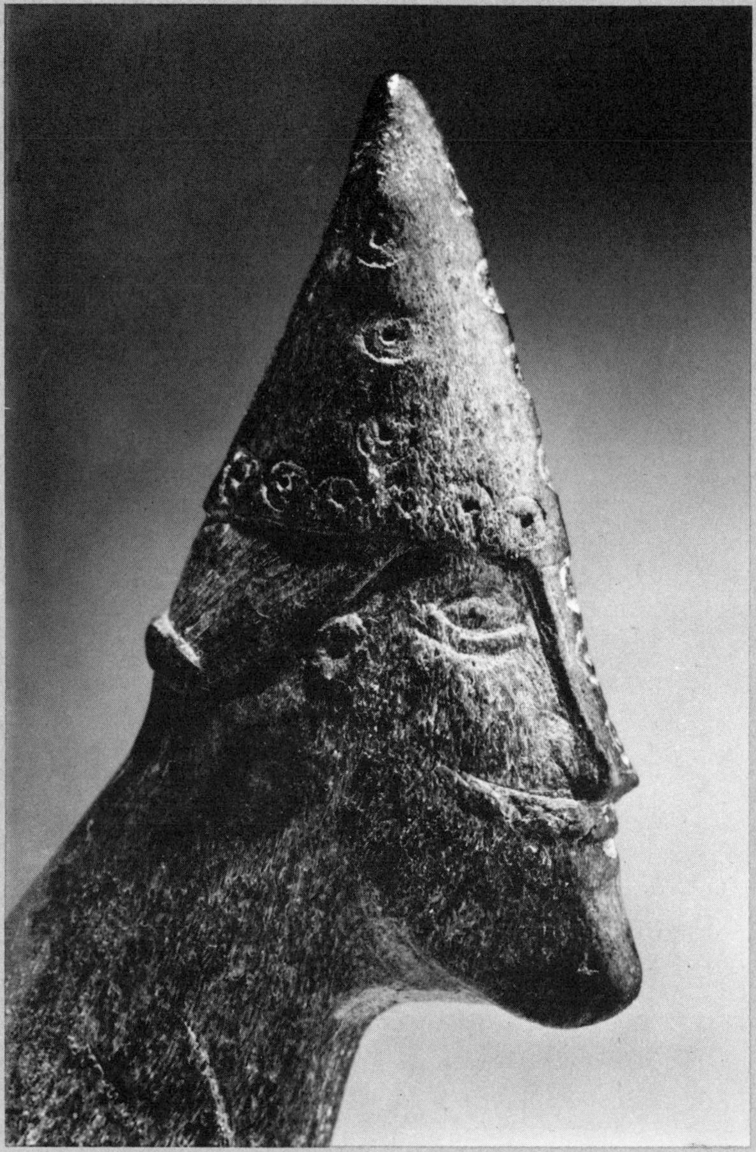

Swedish Vikings traveled over inland water routes to the east in search of trade. They would sail up a river as far as they could, then drag their vessels overland to another river and go on. These adventurers, called Rus, probably gave Russia its name. Swedish Vikings were chosen to serve as the Varingian Guard in Constantinople, capital of the Byzantine empire. These special troops were noted for their loyalty and courage.

A damaged Viking helmet is shown at right, with the remains of a mail shirt. Mail was made of thousands of tiny rings of iron. The rings had to be formed separately out of little bars of iron, then linked one to another. Shirts of mail provided good protection against swords, spears and arrows.

University Museum of
National Antiquities, Oslo

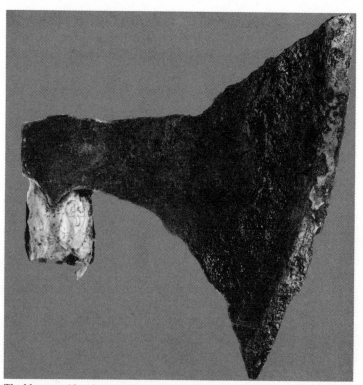

The Museum of London

a Viking warrior always carried his weapons —an ax and a sword—and when he died he was buried with them. The ax at left, with a wide, curving blade, was found with other weapons and tools in England near the old London Bridge over the Thames River. Perhaps it had been lost during a battle around the year 1000, when the Norwegian King Olaf and his troops were attacking the English. Olaf's men rowed their ships under the bridge and tied ropes around the posts that supported it. Then they fastened the other ends of the ropes to their ships and rowed downstream

The National Museum of Denmark

12

as hard as they could. The posts were pulled loose, the bridge collapsed and many Englishmen fell into the river and drowned. The nursery rhyme, "London Bridge Is Falling Down," might be based on this event.

The ax at far left, below, is inlaid with silver wire to form a pattern of animals and plants. To make the inlay, grooves were carved into the surface of the iron, and silver wire was hammered into them.

A Viking's most important weapon was his sword, which he wore in a scabbard, or case, slung from his belt. The gilded silver figure below, left, dressed in a knee-length garment, clasps his sword with both hands. The hilt, or handle, of the sword below, right, is inlaid with copper and silver wires.

Museum of
National Antiquities,
Stockholm

Museum of National Antiquities, Stockholm

The hilt of the sword above is decorated with tiny figures of animals; the blade is long and broad with two cutting edges. A good blade is tough and flexible; it will bend without breaking. Sometimes the hilt and blade of a sword were made by different craftsmen. Viking swords were thought to have magic powers. They were looked upon as trusted friends and were given names.

At left is a bronze chape with an openwork design. A chape protected the tip of a scabbard.

The seven points are arrowheads, which were fitted to wooden shafts and shot by a long, simple bow. The best bows were made from the yew tree.

Shields were round, made of thin, flat wooden boards. In the center was an iron boss, or knob.

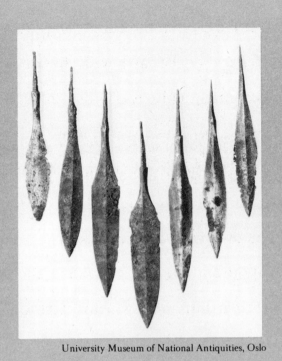

The long blade below is a spearhead. The socket, into which a long wooden shaft fits, is inlaid with silver. Tiny spears were worn as charms. It was said that the first war of the world began when a spear was hurled by Odin. Odin's greatest treasure was his mighty spear Gungnir, made by the dwarves, who were clever in the art of working with metal. If Odin threw Gungnir over a battlefield, the direction it took would show which side would be the victor.

the grass grow. He created the world, set the stars in their courses and lit the earth with the sun. In the Old English language, Odin was known as Woden; a day of our week, Wednesday, is named for him.

Frey was the god of fertility, who sent sunshine and rain and made plants grow. He had a ship that was large enough to carry all the gods, yet could be folded up and put into his bag. His horse, Bloody-hoof, made the earth tremble when its feet touched the ground.

Museum of
National Antiquities,
Stockholm

Historical Museum, University of Bergen, Norway

The tiny bronze figure above, holding spears and a sword and wearing a helmet with horns, may be connected with Odin. Horned helmets had been worn sometimes for ceremonial and magical purposes in earlier times, but Vikings never wore horned helmets.

Odin was the wisest of the Norse gods. He knew all of the secret powers of nature and could hear

The gold charm at left, below, shows Frey in the wheat fields with Gerd, the beautiful daughter of a giant. The charm was probably used in connection with ceremonies to celebrate the growth of crops. It is tiny, less than two inches high. All of these Viking objects made of silver, gold and bronze are small; they were ornaments, worn as jewelry or charms. The little bronze figure at right, above, representing Frey, is only about three inches high.

Museum of National Antiquities, Stockholm

Frey's beautiful twin sister, Freyja, was goddess of love and marriage. She is represented as a pregnant woman in the ornament at right, below. The necklace Freyja is wearing was made for her by the dwarves. These little creatures lived in rocks and in dark caves under the earth. If they came out into the sunlight, they would turn to stone. The necklace that they made for Freyja was once stolen from her by Loki, the mischief maker. He entered her bedroom in the form of a flea while she was asleep and bit her on the neck so that she turned over and he could unfasten her necklace.

Freyja went about in a chariot pulled by white cats. When Freyja wept she shed tears of gold. Friday is named after Freyja.

Museum of National Antiquities, Stockholm

17

Thursday was named for Thor, god of thunder. When Thor shook his red beard, a storm would rage. He had a magic hammer named Mjöllnir, which was made by the dwarves. He used it as a weapon to protect people and gods from his enemies, the giants. This hammer always returned to Thor's hands after he hurled it through the air. Mjöllnir was the greatest of all treasures of the gods. Thor also had a pair of gloves which he wore to pick up huge rocks and shatter them into pieces.

At right is a little bronze statue of Thor holding his hammer. Norsemen wore charms in the form of Thor's hammer for good luck. The one at far right, above, is silver, decorated by two methods of working metal: filigree and granulation. Filigree work is done by laying fine wire threads onto the surface. In granulation, tiny grains of metal form a pattern. The threads and grains are soldered, or joined with melted metal, onto the background.

National Museum of Iceland, Reykjavík

When Thor went about on foot, he could cover the heavens in three steps. He rode to battle in a chariot pulled across the clouds by two billy goats. Thunder rumbled and lightning cracked as he passed. On the bronze brooch below, Thor's goats face each other on either side of a thunderbolt. At one time the brooch had a long pin; it was used to join two sides of a cloak together.

A story is told that Thor once stayed at a farm where there was no food. So he killed his own goats to have meat for supper. When the meal was over, he collected all the bones and placed them on the skins of the goats; the goats came to life again and stood up.

Museum of National
Antiquities, Stockholm

Museum of National
Antiquities, Stockholm

19

The National Museum of Denmark

Historical Museum,
University of Bergen

The Viking Age was a period of great activity in trade. Some of the items the Norsemen

exported, or sent out, were fur, skins, seal oil, walrus teeth and reindeer antlers. They

also sold slaves whom they had captured in war. In return, they imported silks and spices

from the Far East, amber, which is a hard yellowish stone, from the area of the Baltic Sea,

glass from Germany, salt from western Europe and weapons from northern France,

where the best sword blades were made.

Traders bartered merchandise and they also bought and sold goods using silver, which was the standard of exchange. Large quantities of this precious metal came into Scandinavia from Arab mines in western Asia. Silver was valued according to its weight. It was in the form of bars, jewelry, foreign coins, especially Arabic coins, and scraps of metal. Sometimes the coins and the jewelry would be hacked, or cut, into pieces to make up an exact weight. These pieces were called hack silver.

Merchants weighed the silver on a bronze scale, using metal weights for balancing. The scale could be folded up and carried in a little round metal box.

Hoards of silver were sometimes hidden in the earth or under a rock in time of danger. Often the owner did not return, and these treasures that had been buried for a thousand years or more are still being found today.

As time went on the Vikings began to mint, or make, their own coins, which were used as money. A group of Danish coins from the Viking Age is shown between the pans of the balance scale at left. The coins at right are Swedish. The boat represented on the one in the middle is a longship, with shields on display; the boats on the other two coins are knarrs.

Museum of National
Antiquities, Stockholm

The Vikings introduced silver to the Irish and minted the first coins in Ireland. At first the Norsemen had gone to Ireland on raids, bringing back valuable treasures in the form of beautifully decorated metalwork. In time they made settlements there and set up trading centers which later became important cities. The city of Dublin was originally a Viking fortress and trading center.

This wooden gaming board found in Ireland may have been used to play "fox and geese." Pins found with the board would be inserted into the holes to represent the fox and the geese. In the game the fox starts from the center and tries to take the geese; the geese cannot take the

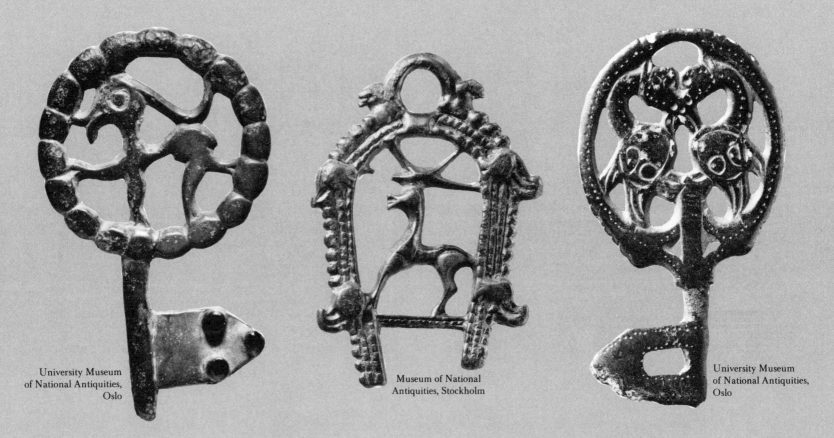

fox, but they try to drive it into a corner from which it cannot escape. Board games were popular among the Norsemen, and chess, which was introduced through trade with the Arab world, was played during late Viking times.

Bronze keys were used to lock boxes and chests in which things were stored. The keys have openwork designs of birds, animals and mythical beasts. The bottom part has broken off from the one in the center, which is decorated with a graceful horned animal. Women wore keys dangling from chains on their chests or hanging from belts, along with their scissors, cases for bone needles, and knives. A large bunch of keys was a sign of a woman's importance.

The favorite animal of the Vikings was the horse, which was often connected with Odin. Odin had a steed with eight legs. According to a legend, a giant had offered to build a wall around Asgard, where the gods lived, to protect them from their enemies. It was agreed that if the giant were to finish the wall in one winter he would get the sun, the moon and the goddess Freyja as payment for the job. The giant worked fast, for he had a clever male horse named Svadilfari that helped him by dragging huge blocks of stone. As winter neared an end, the wall was almost finished. Then Loki thought of a plot to avoid making payment to the giant. He turned himself into a mare; the stallion left his work to run after the mare and the wall was never finished. In time the mare gave birth to a foal with eight legs which was named Sleipner. It became the finest and fastest horse in the world and carried Odin through the clouds.

Horses were sacrificed to the gods by their owners; the flesh of the horse was eaten and its blood drunk as part of the ceremony. Often when a chieftain died, his horse was buried with him.

The little horses above are made of gilded silver. They were sewn onto a woman's dress and found in her grave in Birka, one of the busiest Viking trading centers. Birka is on an island about eighteen miles from the modern city of Stockholm. It was a starting point for one of the trade routes to the east. At Birka the Norsemen exchanged furs—bear, fox, marten, otter and beaver—

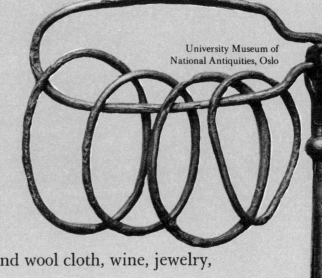

and other merchandise for silver coins, silk and wool cloth, wine, jewelry, glass and weapons.

The Norsemen were skillful ironsmiths. The Viking Age is known as the late Iron Age, for tools and weapons were made of this metal. The iron rattle above was mounted on a sled or wagon. Perhaps the noise it made was expected to keep evil spirits away. The bronze object below was part of a horse's equipment; the reins went through the two large holes.

25

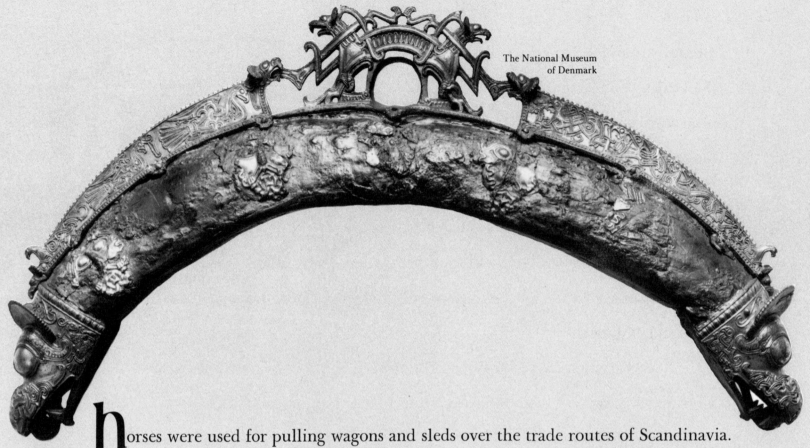

horses were used for pulling wagons and sleds over the trade routes of Scandinavia. In winter iron spikes would be attached to horses' hooves to prevent them from slipping on the ice. Curved wooden harness collars with bronze decorations rested on the backs of the animals and reins were passed through holes in the center. The collar above ends in dragon heads.

Animal heads form the designs on the gold spur and the ornament with it, which was attached to the end of a leather strap. These objects were decorated by filigree and granulation. A rider's equipment was usually plain, but a chieftain could show off his wealth on ceremonial occasions by wearing gold spurs and ornaments.

The gilded bronze objects in the shape of animal heads, at right, decorated a horse's bridle. Animal and bird figures cover the surfaces. These ornaments were found in Gotland, an island off the eastern coast of Sweden, in the Baltic Sea. Gotland was the richest area in Scandinavia. Valuable furs came there from Russia, and other fine goods from Germany and England. Gotland's wealth must have attracted pirates, for hundreds of treasure hoards that had been buried in times of danger have been found there.

University Museum of
National Antiquities, Oslo

Museum of National
Antiquities, Stockholm

27

Many varieties of trees grow in the forests of Scandinavia. Good timber was available for the Norsemen to use in building their houses, as well as their ships. Very few remains of Viking Age houses still exist today, but a model house was constructed in modern times in Trelleborg, Denmark, where a Viking Age military camp once stood. Marks found in the soil showed where upright posts had been set into the ground as a framework for the Viking building. These post holes were used as guides to reconstruct the ground plan. The house-shaped chest below was used as a guide to reconstruct the walls. About three feet away from the walls stands another row of posts, which hold up a roof to protect the walls of the building from rain. The chest and house are shaped something like an upside-down ship, but the ends are straight rather than curved.

Inside, the house is divided into three sections: a large hall in the center for living and sleeping, and smaller rooms at either end for storage. People slept on broad benches that ran the length of the walls. In the center of the great hall was an open fireplace for cooking. Smoke escaped through a hole in the roof, which was the only source of light.

The house-shaped chest was used for storing religious treasures. It is made of wood covered with twenty-two sheets of elk horn and held together by gilded bronze bands. Heads of animals and birds jut out from the sides and ends.

The National Museum of Denmark

and riveted, or joined together with metal nails. The pots hung from chains above the fire. They could be raised or lowered, depending on the amount of heat desired. For cooking outdoors the pot was hung from a stand with three legs, which could be folded up. No cooking could be done aboard ship. If the crew could not go ashore to camp, they ate dried

The silver cup above was found in the grave of a Danish queen. It is decorated with a pattern of animals with ribbonlike bodies entwined around each other.

Everyday bowls and pots in the Viking Age were plain. Pots made of soapstone, a soft whitish stone, and iron or copper kettles were used for cooking. To make the kettle at right, several sheets of iron were heated and hammered out flat, then curved to shape

30

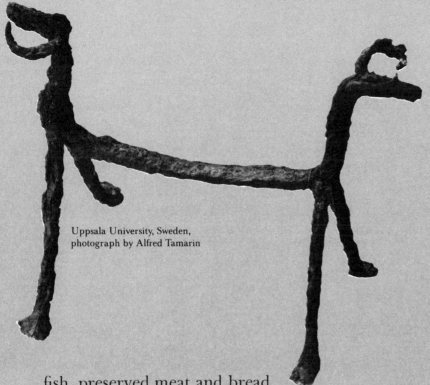

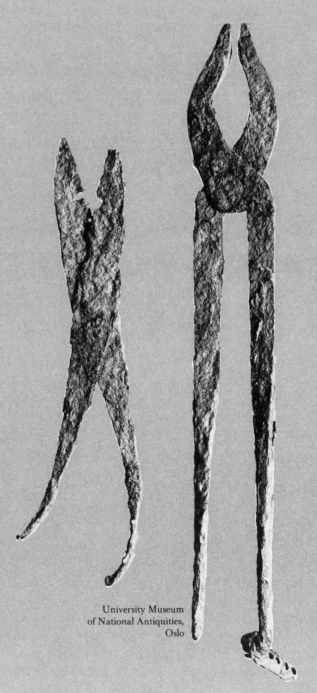

fish, preserved meat and bread,

and they slept on deck in skin sleeping bags.

Above is a fire dog decorated with animal

heads. Fire dogs were used in pairs in an

open fireplace to support burning logs.

Tools used by blacksmiths were not

very different from tools in use today: ham-

mers, tongs, files, chisels and shears. The

shears at near right could cut thin sheets of

metal. The tongs at far right were useful

for handling red-hot iron. Wire could be made

by heating metal and drawing it through

the tiny holes in the handle of the tongs.

Museum of National
Antiquities, Stockholm

Historical Museum,
University of Bergen

Wives of wealthy Gotland merchants wore round box brooches on their shawls. These brooches were so deep they could be used as containers to hold little things such as pieces of silk ribbon. The box brooch at left is made of silver decorated with gold.

The flat object is made of whalebone, carved with horse head figures. It was used for smoothing wrinkles out of linen. The cloth would be placed over it and rubbed rapidly with a round glass ball.

Circular spindle whorls were used in spinning. They were placed as weights on round wooden rods which were twirled around as the wool was drawn out into yarn. Archaeologists found the soapstone spindle whorl at right, above, in the remains of a Viking settlement in L'Anse aux Meadows in northern Newfoundland, Canada.

Norse sagas, or stories, tell of the settling of Greenland and the discovery of North America.

These sagas were passed along by word of mouth for hundreds of years, then written down by poets in Iceland in the thirteenth and fourteenth centuries. They describe how Eric the Red, a native of Norway, left his Viking settlement in Iceland and sailed to Greenland, where he formed a colony in the year 982. Four years later another Norwegian, Bjarni Herjolfsson, went to Iceland looking for his parents, only to learn that they had gone to Greenland with Eric the Red. Following them, Bjarni was blown off course and driven southwest until he saw an unfamiliar coastline, with wooded hills. He did not go ashore, but a few years later Leif, son of Eric the Red, bought Bjarni's boat and set off with thirty-five men to this unknown land. When he reached the coast, he followed it south, landed and spent the winter. Then in spring he sailed for home. Later Leif Ericson's brother, Thorvald, explored the new continent even further, but was killed by Eskimos or Indians. According to the sagas, there were other Viking expeditions over the years.

Norse objects and sites of Viking houses recently found in L'Anse aux Meadows are the first proof that Vikings landed in America hundreds of years before Columbus.

The spindle whorl at right is engraved with runes, the earliest kind of writing in Scandinavia.

Historical Museum,
University of Bergen

33

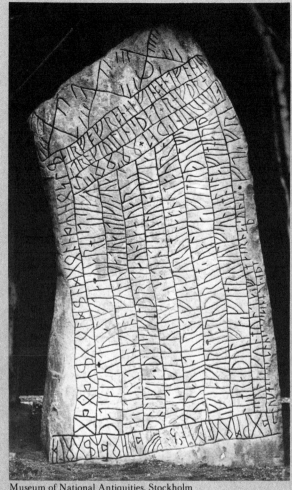

Museum of National Antiquities, Stockholm

The Vikings had an alphabet of sixteen runes, or characters. The runes are made up almost entirely of straight strokes and were used for carving messages on hard surfaces, especially stone and wood.

Large stones carved with runic inscriptions were set up to protect the dead and honor their memory. The runes on the stones name the dead person, the one who had the stone set up and sometimes the man who did the carving. Often they tell how and where the person died, whether in battle or in a peaceful occupation, and express the wish that he or she will enjoy the grave. Sometimes they praise the dead person's courage, faith or generosity, or tell of an important event or a good deed done by a person still alive.

This stone in Sweden contains about 800 runes, not all of which can be deciphered.

In later times pictures were carved on memorial stones. Harald Bluetooth, a Danish king who ruled from about 940 to 985, erected the gray granite stone at right in memory of his parents. Runes on the stone tell of Harald's achievements as king and that he won all of Denmark and Norway and made the Danes Christian. A figure of Christ is surrounded by a pattern of interlocking rings. The Danes were the first Scandinavians to become Christian. Christianity came to Norway early in the eleventh century, and to Sweden some years later.

The National Museum
of Denmark

Museum of National Antiquities, Stockholm

Picture stones from Gotland show scenes of gods and men fighting in battle, in this life and the hereafter. In the lower part of this dead nobleman's stone, his longship, with a square sail, glides over the ocean waves. Above that the hero, carrying a shield, is riding his horse to the next world.

He is going to Valhalla, the hall of Odin where champions who had died in battle spent their days fighting in the meadows. In the evening all who had been killed on the battlefield that day would rise up unharmed to join in a feast served by the Valkyries and drink mead, a beverage made with honey. The Valkyries were maidens who watched over battles on earth and summoned the bravest of the warriors who died to Valhalla. From his throne at Valhalla Odin could look out over all creation. His two ravens flew about the world all day and returned in the evening to perch on his shoulder and tell him what was going on.

On the stone Sleipner, Odin's eight-legged horse, carries a fallen warrior to Valhalla. Behind Sleipner three men are walking with their swords pointed down, a sign of death. In the top section a battle is in progress. A warrior has been knocked off his horse by a man wielding a sword; to the left, two men holding swords seem to be swearing an oath. Eagles and men fill the sky. According to mythology, an eagle sat on the World Tree, the mighty ash at the center of the universe that held the earth in place and supported the sky. From this special seat the eagle could view the entire universe.

The stone at right is carved with two men in a small sailboat. The man in the stern is steering the boat with the rudder. Above them the large figure of a bearded warrior wearing a pointed helmet and baggy trousers and carrying a round shield is riding to Valhalla. A Valkyrie holding a horn drinking cup filled with mead greets him.

Museum of National Antiquities, Stockholm

A Valkyrie carrying a drinking horn is represented in the small silver ornament at near right. She is wearing a long dress and bracelets and neck rings. The woman in silver at far right has long hair tied in a knot at the back of her head and hanging in a pigtail. She is wearing a dress that trails on the ground and a shawl with a design of dots. Dresses and cloaks were not sewn to fit; a rectangle of cloth was draped around the body and held together with pins or brooches.

Museum of National
Antiquities, Stockholm

It was the fashion for a woman to wear an apron over her linen dress. The apron was held up by straps over the shoulders, which were fastened with two brooches, usually oval in shape. Strings of beads or fine chains hung from these brooches.

Another bronze ornament, often trefoil, or three-leafed, in shape, would be pinned between the oval brooches. This one is covered with a design of animal faces and long, twisting shapes that intertwine. Viking artists liked to cover every possible space with designs. Bronze keys were often hung from the trefoil brooches. The idea of trefoil objects with things hanging from them came from France, where they were worn by men.

The silver brooch below, with animal figures looking backward, was used to fasten the edges of a cape or cloak together.

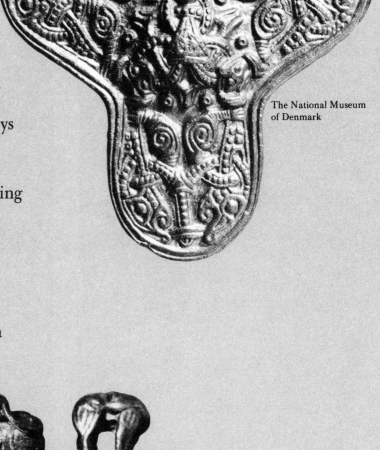

The National Museum
of Denmark

Historical Museum,
University of Bergen

Oval brooches worn in pairs to hold up the straps of an apron were called tortoise brooches because of their shape. An iron pin fastened them onto the cloth. The tortoise brooch at left has figures of smiling beasts with large round eyes and pigtails trailing from their heads; their hind paws grasp their necks and front paws grasp each other. Other "gripping beast" figures form the border.

Tortoise brooches were often produced in quantity. They were made by casting, an ancient method for working metal. A clay mold was made in the shape of the object, and melted metal was poured into it. When the metal cooled, it turned hard; then the object could be removed from the mold and polished.

The gripping beasts with long, twisting bodies and bald heads at right, above, were carved from jet,

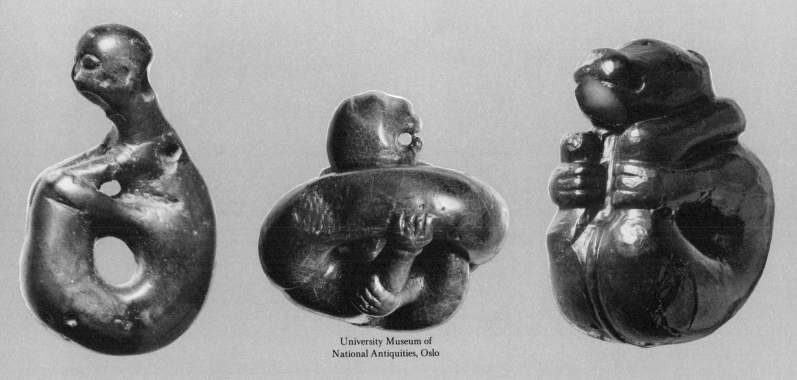

a hard, shiny black form of natural carbon which came from England.

A group of standing animals gathered around a little house decorates the round silver brooch below, which was used to pin the ends of a cloak together. The figures on top of the brooch would have been cast separately and riveted onto the surface.

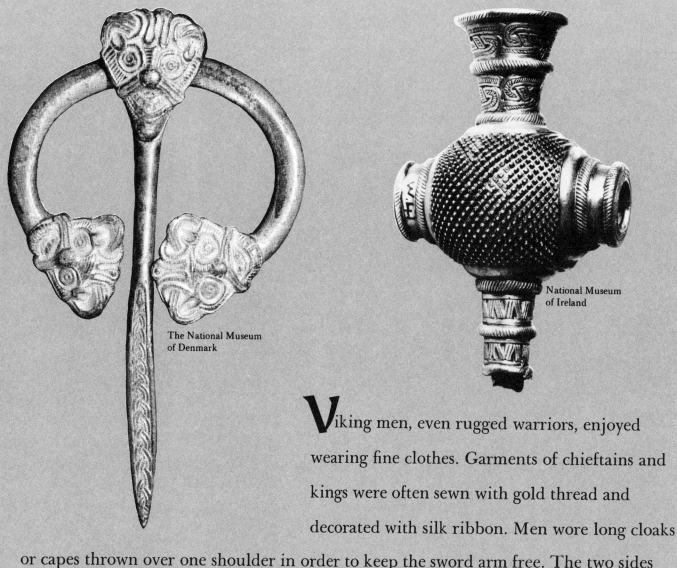

The National Museum
of Denmark

National Museum
of Ireland

Viking men, even rugged warriors, enjoyed wearing fine clothes. Garments of chieftains and kings were often sewn with gold thread and decorated with silk ribbon. Men wore long cloaks or capes thrown over one shoulder in order to keep the sword arm free. The two sides of the cloak were fastened at the shoulder by a penannular brooch, a long pin with a ring that held it in place. The silver object shaped like a thistle above, right, comes from Ireland and was once the top of a penannular brooch. The thistle is so large that the ring of the brooch must have measured about ten inches across and the pin about two feet long. The Irish passed a law that pins should not be too long, for they could be a danger. Human heads decorate the ring on the pin above, found in a woman's grave.

Men as well as women wore bracelets and also rings of gold and silver. Kings gave gold rings as gifts to those who fought most bravely. Poems were written in praise of this practice.

According to legend, Odin gave gold rings to his followers. A gold ring named Draupnir that constantly multiplied was one of Odin's treasures. Every ninth night, nine new gold rings would drop from it. An arm ring that was said to have belonged to Thor was kept in a temple, and oaths were sworn on it. The person who wore it was thought to be protected from sword blows.

The silver bracelet at right, above, has a pattern of deep grooves and a beaded design. The neck ring below it was made by intertwining rods of twisted silver with fine twisted silver thread.

The National Museum of Denmark

Historical Museum,
University of Bergen

43

Viking craftsmen made jewelry in many different shapes. The bronze brooch at right is in the form of a ship with a dragon head on the prow. Dragon heads were set up when Vikings sailed against the enemy, but were taken down when they sailed home so that the good guardian spirits of the country would not be frightened away.

The round brooch at left has a design of four human heads and little animals between them. It is made of silver and gilded.

Silver was plentiful during the Viking Age but gold was scarce. Only small objects, such as finger rings, could be made entirely of gold. And gilding was popular. One method of gilding is to apply a mixture of gold and mercury to an object and heat it until the mercury volatizes, or evaporates, leaving a coating of gold.

At right is a large bronze weather vane that is gilded. It has an openwork design of a great beast fighting with a serpent. The details, or fine lines, were engraved. Engraving, in which the artist uses a sharp-edged tool to make deep lines in the surface of the metal, is one of the most common methods of metalwork. An animal that was cast separately stands on top of the vane, which was found in a church. It originally had been made for a ship and possibly had been used on a vessel in Cnut's fleet. Cnut was Danish. His father, Swein Forkbeard, was a Viking king who conquered England. The son, known as Cnut the Great, ruled Denmark and Norway and became king of England in 1016. His laws were fair and people had their rights. The Vikings have always believed in freedom and equality.

Museum of National
Antiquities, Stockholm

45

When the Vikings accepted Christianity, they built wooden structures that were called stave churches because the walls were made of upright staves, or planks. At left is the stave church at Borgund, in western Norway, which was built in the twelfth century. It has several steep roofs, one above the other, covered with shingles, thin pieces of wood laid in overlapping rows. Carved wooden dragons were thought to prevent evil spirits from entering the church. The fact that crosses and dragon heads appear on the same building shows a mixture of Viking and early Christian beliefs.

This beautiful wood carving is on the wall of a stave church at Urnes, also in western Norway. A twisting serpent is entwined around a slender stag gnawing on a plant. According to mythology, a huge serpent was coiled around the earth and at the foot of the World Tree. Beneath the roots of the tree was a spring which was the source of wisdom, guarded by a wise giant of the underworld.

Photograph by
Alfred Tamarin

Photograph University
Museum of National
Antiquities, Oslo

It took two centuries for the Scandinavians to give up belief in their own traditions and mythology and to accept Christianity. Even while the new religion was slowly winning acceptance, many Norsemen clung to their old gods. Often people wore crosses along with hammers of Thor and other symbols of the Norse gods.

By the end of the eleventh century, the Scandinavians had lost their power at sea. They gave up their sailing expeditions and settled down.

The new ideas that the Vikings had learned in their travels were brought home to become part of their own ways. With these ideas, Norse culture slowly changed. In time the culture of the three Scandinavian kingdoms—Norway, Sweden and Denmark—became part of the general European culture of the Middle Ages.

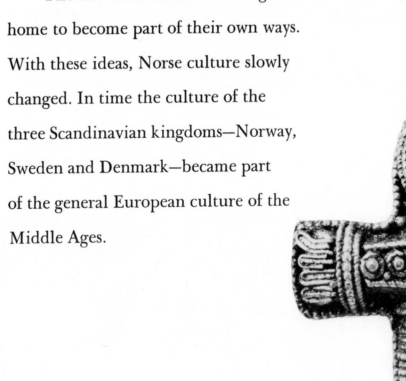

Museum of
National Antiquities,
Stockholm